WOODEN BOATS
From Sculls to Yachts

WOODEN BOATS
From Sculls to Yachts

Joseph Gribbins

Introduction by Jon Wilson

Friedman Group

A FRIEDMAN GROUP BOOK

Copyright © 1991 by Michael Friedman Publishing Group, Inc.

ISBN 0-8021-1404-0

WOODEN BOATS
From Sculls to Yachts
was prepared and produced by
Michael Friedman Publishing Group, Inc.
15 West 26th Street
New York, New York 10010

Editor: Stephen Williams
Designer: Judy Morgan
Photography Editor: Christopher C. Bain

Typeset by Miller & Debel Typographers
Color separation by United South Sea Graphic Art Co., Ltd.
Printed and bound in Hong Kong by Leefung-Asco Printers Ltd.

Dedication

To the summer residents of Scudders Falls, New Jersey, whose
wooden boats gave me such pleasure as a boy.

Acknowledgements

The author wishes to thank Peter Spectre, Jon Wilson, Paul Lipke,
and Phil Bolger for advice and encouragement in the course of
working up the text of this book. And all the photographers who
provided such stunning images for these pages. And most of all the
owners, restorers, and lovers of these boats.

CONTENTS

INTRODUCTION

The sculptural qualities of most wooden boats are a large part of their magic. At right, a shapely little catboat, unrigged and at rest, in the Cutts & Case boatyard on the eastern shore of Maryland.

There are many sailors who insist that wooden boats have soul; that, unlike their mass-produced sisters, they are truly living beings. For the uninitiated, it is easy to be skeptical of such conceits, and to dismiss them as merely romantic notions. But romance is not infatuation; it is the engagement of heart and mind, and there are few contrivances as utterly engaging as boats built of wood. There is something profoundly important in the fashioning of timbers and planks for yachts and boats; something very spiritual in the shaping of the material. Perhaps it has to do with ancient things: a blending of ancient skills with an ancient resource. Or perhaps it has to do with the honor of transforming something so grand and graceful as a tree into something so lithe and lovely as a boat. Certainly there are few opportunities in life these days to blend art, science, and the natural world in so dramatic a fashion.

The old tradition of the boatbuilder going into a stand of oaks to find the perfect trees for keel and frame, into a cedar swamp for the finest planking, and to his special stack of cherry or butternut for interior wood-work that will radiate warmth and color, is passing away. Few builders harvest their own timber anymore. Yet, like all artisans, each selects his stock with the keenest eye: this straight-grained spruce for spars that will carry a cloud of canvas; this elbow crook of apple for seat knees in the rowing tender. The relationship between the boatbuilder and his medium is not unlike that between the luthier and his. They think not only of the grain and figure of the wood, but of its age; indeed, each prefers not only old-growth wood, but wood that has aged after cutting: the older, the better. As if the wisdom of the wood is better expressed with age.

Details that represent ingenuity and crafts-manship are another attraction for owners and admirers of good wooden boats. Here is the laid-strip afterdeck and boomkin of a Chesapeake Bay log canoe.

© Eric Poggenpohl

It's an appealing notion, the possibility that there is wisdom in a wooden boat. It is not so far-fetched. After all, what is wisdom but the accumulation and absorption of skill and experience? And what is the art of boatbuilding but the application of skill and experience? When builders hew their timbers with axe and adze, and shape their planks with saw and plane, they bring both wisdom and love to their art. As they fasten keel and frames together for the skeleton, and fit planks upon it for the skin, they are doing nothing so much as creating a new life. And with each new piece the life grows more distinct. To witness the construction of a wooden boat is to witness a remarkable transformation: an evolution of extraordinary dimension. One might say that every kind of construction is equally miraculous, and so it is. But it is this particular working of natural materials with ancient skills to create timeless forms that engages me so totally. Indeed, it is the access to this process that makes it so engaging. Most of us could not in a lifetime construct an automobile in our back yards. Nor even, for that matter, a fiberglass boat. The technologies are capital-intensive, and complex. Yet, with patience and a modicum of skill, many of us might construct the boat of our dreams within sight of the window over the kitchen sink. In a world where the pace of technology outstrips our ability to respond and relate, we need to touch these elements, lest we lose our sense of wonder at these gifts.

Fortunately, there seems to be a wooden boat for nearly every taste and temperament. From antique to modern, sail to power, slow to fast, small to large, the varieties are endless. There are builders who specialize in a lightweight wooden canoe one could raise overhead with one hand. There are shipyards that still build ocean-going wooden minesweepers for the United States Navy. There are workboat builders, yacht builders, skiff and speedboat builders who choose wood consciously. They prefer the way it works as it goes together, the way it floats in its element, and the way it can be repaired in the most out-of-the-way places on earth. They love the way it feels under their hands and the way it behaves underway. They love how it bends into graceful forms, and won't be forced into awkward and clumsy shapes. They love how it seems to work with them and not against them. And somehow, these builders continue to survive our high-tech and fast times. Indeed, there is even a construction method for the times, which has allowed the art and science of wooden boatbuilding to advance comfortably into the twenty-first century. So the future seems secure. Unlike the petrochemical resins from which fiberglass boats are manufactured, the resource from which wooden boats are built has a chance at perpetuation: Wood is the earth's only renewable construction resource, and it asks only that we husband it with foresight and care.

In many ways, wooden boats symbolize the potential of man's ability to transform and create at an elemental level. And such symbols deserve at least some measure of respect. We are fortunate that Joe Gribbins has elected to share his own sense of the uniqueness of wooden boats. There are few as experienced as Joe at shaping an inspiring picture. His understanding of the intricacies of all manner of boats, words, and pictures makes this work a virtual celebration of the varieties of wooden boats—a feast for all of us who love the rich relationships of wood and water.

Jon Wilson

Editor, *WoodenBoat* magazine

One virtue of wooden boats is the history they represent. These English rowing skiffs are the same boats that took the rat and the mole on their adventures in Kenneth Grahame's The Wind in the Willows, and their fine lines go back to the Vikings.

BEAUTY AND TRUTH

The truth of wooden boats—
the integrity we sense
beneath the beauty—reveals
itself in the way the boats
are made, in the clever
things boat builders have
done for ages, and in the
dead-practical details
of the boats.

One of the most familiar types of wooden boats in the world is the canvas-covered cedar canoe—like the one in the bulrushes on the opposite page. These are wooden adaptations of the birchbark canoes built by the Algonquins of the United States and Canada. On the previous two pages is one of Martin Marine's new recreational rowing shells.

BEAUTY AND TRUTH ARE INTERTWINED, AS JOHN KEATS TELLS US IN HIS "Ode on a Grecian Urn." But with wooden boats, the beauty is more obvious than the truth, as you can see in these photographs. The truth of wooden boats—the integrity we sense beneath the beauty—reveals itself in the way the boats are made, in the clever things boat builders have done for ages, and in the dead-practical details of the boats. From the strong bitt on the foredeck of a working vessel to the curve in the coach roof of a little yacht that makes stand-up headroom possible down below, great care is taken to ensure that design complements function. And we see beauty and truth together in such finishing touches as the plain paint work of boats that get knocked around a lot, in the rakish windshield of a mahogany speedboat, in the bare teak on the deck of a boat that goes to sea, put there to give the surest footing when the decks are wet.

Wooden boats are a complex of good ideas and attractive shapes and surfaces that we appreciate on sight, whether we know what they're all about or not. When we know more about boats—and become familiar with the way they work and move, and when we fix them and refinish them over time—our appreciation gets deeper. Wooden boats can become almost mystical things to some people, and the relationship between people and their boats is definitely romantic.

Nearly every one of the boats in this book represents a fond and complex attachment between an otherwise sensible human being and something wonderful made out of wood. Each one of

Another type of canoe, originally English, is the all-wood decked canoe, normally finished bright and propelled like a kayak with a double paddle. Popular all over the world in the late nineteenth century, decked wooden canoes are now having a revival.

© Neil Rabinowitz

the boats here is beautiful, and each one is true to the principles of how it is meant to be used, how it is put together, how it will satisfy its owner in a complex of ways. Each one is capable of inspiring—yes!—a relationship.

People involved with boats made out of stuff other than wood—which is nearly everybody on the waterfront—make jokes about "the wooden-boat religion," and *Nautical Quarterly* once published an article about the revival of interest in wooden boats subtitled *more than a reaction, less than a religion.* But this waterfront joking about wooden boats and the people who care for them frequently masks admiration. Wooden boats for the most part *are* beautiful; they *do* represent great human ingenuity and workmanship; and most of their custodians and lovers *do* spend truly devotional

© Christopher Bain

Floating sports cars, the varnished mahogany runabouts that were built by the tens of thousands from roughly 1920 to 1960 are having their own revival. Like these examples, they tend to be restored and polished to showroom-new shine.

© Christopher Bain

17

Another sporty type, the wood-hulled racing
sailboat, has survived fiberglass and the
volatile politics of sailboat racing to become a
classic. Old campaigners like the 1930s Twelve
Meter shown here under sail and the log canoe
seen at rest are sometimes raced,
always admired.

amounts of time, money, and labor to bring them to high standards of beauty and truth and keep them there. Owners of fiberglass and aluminum boats—really just mass-produced floating major appliances—can't help but admire wooden boats. The newer boats they own and use but don't necessarily love are boats in body but not in soul.

People who own other types of boats can't help wondering about the owners of wooden boats, those true believers whose passion was described in *Nautical Quarterly* as "irrational and inordinate" and whose special gift was described as "an ability to ignore the advice of their accountants." Small and uncomplicated wooden boats may call for the first of these qualities, but normally not the second; larger wooden boats—cruisers, motor yachts, most cruising sailboats—definitely require both. But as artifacts of a truly premodern age, and often as works of art, wooden boats deserve such devotion.

THE RISE AND FALL OF WOODEN BOATS

The revival of interest in—and, indeed, the passion for—wooden boats is a recent phenomenon. A single note will put it in perspective. Jimmy Potter, now a partner in a boat-restoration shop near Ottawa, Ontario, in Canada, grew up with his family's wooden boats on a stretch of the Rideau River where vessels ranging from cedar canoes to mahogany launches abounded in thousands between 1900 and 1960. In a book published by Ottowa's Manotick Classic Boat Club, *On a Sunday Afternoon*, Potter wrote, "In 1965, when fiberglass boats were so popular, there were only three or four mahogany speedboats on the Long Reach. By 1975, the interest in wooden boats had increased to a point where the Manotick Classic Boat Club was formed, later becoming a chapter of an international society with over 3,100 members and some 10,000 boats."

A classic small wooden boat that never went out of style is the Adirondack guideboat shown above. Guideboats a hundred years old are still in use all over the North Country of New York State, and new examples are still being built.

This sudden death and resurrection of wooden boats is what happened to a greater or lesser extent all over the United States and Canada in the sixties and seventies. (The resurgence of interest in old boats, though not the death of them in the first place, has taken place in other parts of the world, such as Australia, France, Germany, England, and Scandinavia.) Wooden boats were replaced in the sixties and seventies by fiberglass boats and to a small extent by aluminum boats, which began to be produced in quantity during the fifties. The new boats were easier to care for—no painting, varnishing, or rot—and they did nearly everything the old wooden boats did. And they were new, like the Oldsmobile Delta 88 in the driveway. They had the attraction of something fresh and seamless and uncomplicated. And if the truth be told, some of them— like Bertram Yacht's legendary 31-foot (9.5-meter) sportfishing boat, the fiberglass speedboats and small cruisers produced by Chris-Craft and Glasspar, and even the utilitarian boats made by Boston Whaler—were good-looking and well-behaved.

The new boats replaced the old boats very quickly on the Rideau River and elsewhere, and fiberglass and aluminum boats continue to outnumber wooden boats by a huge margin. The old wooden boats were put aside in yards and barns, burned to ashes, or sold to less-affluent types who couldn't afford something new. Kids bought the old speedboats, and working stiffs and romantics bought the old cruisers and cruising sailboats, and they did their best to care for them with house paint and fiberglass cloth and window putty. A boatyard owner I know bulldozed a dozen old cruisers into the ground in the late sixties when the yard bills went unpaid and he needed the space they were taking up. In the seventies, an old-boat lover I know went to see about a forties-era Chris-Craft cruiser that he thought might be for sale and discovered that it had been put to the torch the week before. In my childhood, I was given a twenties-era outboard

Hard use and no particular reverence for craftsmanship and style remain the lot of some wooden-boat types, especially workboats. The beached lobsterboat and the rowing skiff rentals shown here are appropriate examples.

© Christopher Bain

© Christopher Bain

© Allan Weitz

Some wooden boats do elite work—and they look the part. This 100-pound (45-kg) yacht tender, designed by the great Murray Peterson to serve his traditional schooner yachts, combines function with furniture finish.

hydroplane and took it apart to get the brass screws and mahogany out of it for other projects.

Old boats then were thought to be just plain old. They were irrelevant, even pointless. It was as if all the wooden furniture in your house, from deal tables to mahogany highboys, had suddenly been replaced with plastic replicas that promised to be easier to live with. And after they were gone—burned in the fireplace, sold in yard sales, stowed away in the garage—you were happy to be rid of them. They were a nuisance, after all. Soulful, perhaps, but a nuisance nonetheless.

KEEPING THE FAITH

What happened to beauty and truth during those years? you might ask, reacting to the sacrilege of both Sheraton secretaries and Herreshoff launches reduced to ashes or rot. The answer is hard to explain. The good news is that it didn't happen to antique wooden furniture. The bad news is that it did happen to a lot of antique wooden boats. While there were some people who kept the faith and held on to their wooden boats because they were attached to them; who liked painting, varnishing, and replacing rotted wood; or who couldn't afford or didn't want the new, "improved" models, others weren't so fortunate. By the 1970s these unfortunates were beginning to miss the old boats.

One of them, a successful man who had pressed his nose against the windows of the Elco showroom in Manhattan as a kid in the twenties and had dreamed ever since of owning one of the gleaming cruisers inside, bought a 38-foot (11.5-meter) Elco built in 1929. It was in reasonably good shape, and its restoration was expected to cost eight thousand to twelve thousand dollars. But the dream was stronger than the advice of the man's accountant, and the restoration work

One of the most numerous wooden-workboat types in the world is the lobster boat, used for lobstering, scalloping, and a few other fisheries in New England and Canada. These boats (this page and opposite) are still built in wood, especially in Canada's Maritime Provinces, and they combine usefulness, ruggedness, and a plain beauty all their own.

© Christopher Bain

lasted three years and cost one hundred and fifty thousand dollars. Needless to say, the boat finished up as perfect as she had been in the Elco showroom.

Another old-boat connoisseur, a boatyard owner in New Jersey, acquired a 34-foot (10.4-meter) Elco in 1970 to settle a yard bill. He put three years of restoration time into the boat in his own shop and estimated that the cost would have been fifty thousand dollars if he had sent himself a bill. When the job was done he told his wife, "Don't mention Elco to me ever again." But a little while later he bought a 42-foot (almost 13-meter) Elco that needed work. The final illustrative story is of Jimmy Potter, the man who wrote so eloquently of the disappearance of mahogany speedboats on his stretch of Canada's Rideau River. Potter found his father's old Peterborough

runabout in 1965, in sad shape, with a bar stool for a seat and slathered with house paint. But he

began a restoration that led ultimately to a new career as the proprietor of a boat-restoration shop.

These are typical tales of the wooden-boat revival—more than a reaction, less than a religion.

These rescued and restored boats joined the small legion of wooden boats that made it through

the gloomy decades when fiberglass and aluminum were ascendant. In certain places—Maine,

the Carolinas, the Pacific Northwest—wooden boats were still being built in the sixties and

seventies, with perhaps the principal examples being Maine lobster boats turned out with white

cedar planking on oak frames by dozens of small shops. And elite wooden yachts were still built

for people who could afford the upkeep of wood and revered the old traditions; these were sometimes built by the same Maine yards that turned out the lobster boats. And many of the people who could afford the upkeep of wood and revered the old traditions never abandoned their old boats, some of them built fifty years before. At the other end of the economic scale were wooden-workboat proprietors who couldn't afford anything else, the principal examples being the crabbers and oyster harvesters of Chesapeake Bay. And there were hundreds of amateur builders of rowing boats, small sailboats, and outboard utility boats. Some of these backyard boatwrights represented a continuation of the plywood-kit-boat phenomenon of the fifties; others were people who built their own little boats because it was cheaper than buying something new in aluminum or fiberglass; a number were real craftsmen who wanted a traditional boat built in the traditional way.

A NEW ERA

These last were inspired by John Gardner, a historian, professional boat builder, and traditional-small-boat evangelist who wrote a monthly column in the sixties and seventies for a fishing-industry newspaper called *National Fisherman*, and who became the curator of small boats and master of the boat-building shop at Mystic Seaport in Connecticut. John Gardner almost singlehandedly revived interest in such traditional small-boat types as dories, Whitehall boats, Maine's Rangeley Lakes boats, sharpies, and peapods, not only in North America but throughout the world.

A lot of lively things were happening to the allegedly dead traditions of wooden-boat ownership and construction by the middle of the seventies, despite the dominance of other materials in the marketplace. Beauty and truth were not forgotten, and roughly thirty years after boats

In a very real sense, a good small boat is a piece of waterfront furniture. This varnished Adirondack guideboat, with its wicker seat and seatback for the comfort of a fisherman casting for bass, represents several kinds of furniture.

The evolution of rowing boats for speed can be seen in these two photos. The elegant English rowing skiffs below are stable, relatively fast, and meant for holiday excursions. The competition rowing shell at right is very fast, unstable, and meant for pure speed. The rowing skiff is its distant ancestor.

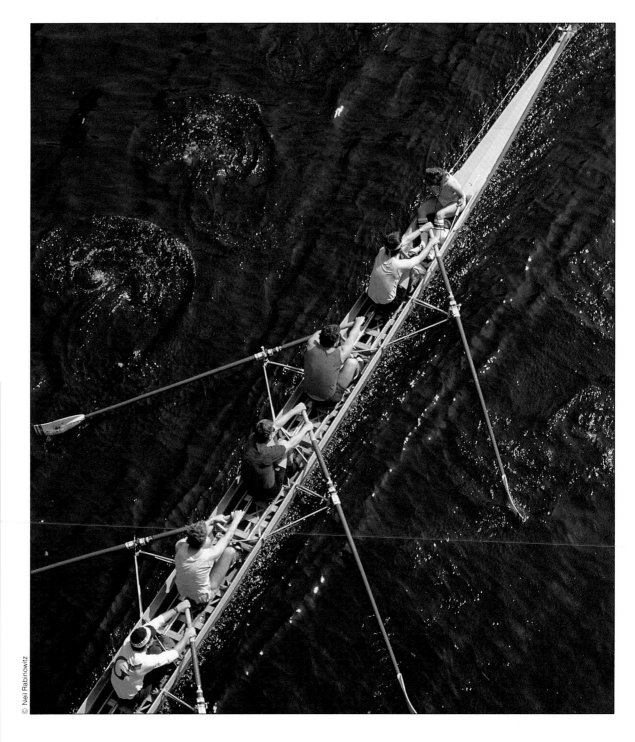

Nearly all wooden boats are examples of artistry, whether deliberately or not. Traditional types tend to be an unconscious blend of style and substance. Newer types tend to be more designed. Ravelston, *shown here, a commuter cruiser drawn by the great John Hacker in 1939, is one of the most stunning powerboats in the world.*

began to be manufactured rather than made by hand, there was enough interest in wooden boats—old boats, restored boats, new boats built in the old way—that the phenomenon began to be more organized. The world's first antique-boat show was organized in the mid-1960s by what was soon to become the Thousand Islands Shipyard Museum in Clayton, New York, and it was to inspire many other antique-boat gatherings. The Antique and Classic Boat Society was established in 1975 in Lake George, New York, and has grown in the years since to an organization of five thousand members and thirty-four chapters from Canada to Florida to Southern California. That same year, Captain Melbourne Smith, an artist and boat-builder, talked the city of Baltimore into building the first *Pride of Baltimore,* a historic replica that was the first of a recent fleet of new wooden vessels, large and small, built all over the world to re-create the nautical past. In 1970, Connecticut's Mystic Seaport convened the first of its Small Craft Workshops, an annual gathering of traditional small rowing and sailing boats, most of them built by their owners, presided over by the legendary John Gardner. In the late 1960s, Dick Wagner of Seattle began to rent wooden sailing and rowing boats on Lake Union, in the heart of the city, and by the 1970s found himself selling traditional wooden boats from his Old Boathouse to people all over the country. His operation was the inspiration for the Traditional Wooden Boat Society on the West Coast and for Seattle's Center for Wooden Boats. In 1972, Lance Lee established the first of his two Apprenticeshops in Maine, set up to build traditional small boats in the traditional way, to sail and work them, and to teach attitudes of craftsmanship and ancient, down-to-earth values. In 1974, *WoodenBoat* magazine made a modest beginning as a publication celebrating wooden boats and their heritage, and serving owners of wooden boats with everything from practical tips to esoteric information about wood, things it still does wonderfully from offices in a waterfront mansion in Brooklin, Maine. The wooden-boat revival was acquiring depth as well as breadth.

Meanwhile there were clubs for owners and fans of everything from classic canoes to ancient racing yachts—including the Traditional Small Craft Society, the Port Elco Club, the Antique Outboard Racing Association, the Wooden Boat Foundation, the Catboat Association, the Chris-Craft Antique Boat Club, and the Great Lakes Wooden Sailboat Society.

Today there are well-established communities of wooden-boat enthusiasts in the United States and Canada, England, France, and elsewhere, whose organizations represent—and, indeed, revere—nearly every type of wooden boat imaginable, large and small, ancient and modern,

Wooden boats have their shrines—boatyards devoted to wood craftsmanship in both restoration work and new construction. There are more of them all the time, along with old-boat clubs, antique-boat shows, and traditional-boat publications. One of the great wooden-boat yards is Cutts & Case in Oxford, Maryland, shown below.

© Eric Poggenpohl

Races and cruises for certain types of wooden boats are on the increase as well. Chesapeake Bay log canoes, shown below, race every summer, as they have for many decades, and new boats join this venerable fleet from time to time. At left, Concordia yawls cruise in company during a recent rendezvous.

Sailing workboats were once the commonest type of working craft in the United States, Canada, and Europe. There are still some boats that carry freight or catch fish under sail in places like Egypt, China, Indonesia, and Chile; but the only fleet of working sail left in the United States is in Chesapeake Bay, where skipjacks like those shown here dredge for oysters.

© Eric Poggenpohl

elite and down-to-earth. In places where wooden boats flourished before the 1960s, they are flourishing again.

The wooden-boat revival—perhaps a preposterous idea in the early 1960s, when old boats were being abandoned, burned, taken apart, sold for whatever they would fetch—is nothing less than a phenomenon. There is a reason for it, and the boats in this book bear witness to the reason. These things are beautiful, and in a time when a sophisticated worldwide culture shares all the information of the ages, nearly as much new data, and probably no more wisdom than there ever was, wooden boats represent a kernel of ancient, made-by-hand, designed-by-eye, loved-like-an-heirloom truth.

Uffa Fox, that legendary English boat designer and builder of wooden boats, put it in perspective in commenting on some carvings on the King of England's yacht *Britannia:* "How well the carver loved his work, and the hours spent at it one can only imagine, for this age, with its acceptance of articles stamped out by machines in thousands, has lost one of the greatest joys of life—the joy of working quietly with the hands and brain alone."

THE HISTORY OF WOODEN BOATS

Evidence suggests that building boats from pieces of wood began with the Egyptians, although dugouts with rough planks pegged or lashed on to build up the sides or added to the central hull in the form of outriggers are more ancient than we will ever know.

On the preceding page are traditional rowing boats at Seattle's Center for Wooden Boats, a place where visitors can rent great old boats to row on Lake Union. On the opposite page is a Tancook Whaler replica built recently by Lance Lee's Apprenticeshop in Rockport, Maine. The Apprenticeshop teaches boatbuilding and many other skills; the Center for Wooden Boats rents old boats, sells replicas of traditional types, and has been a focus of the wooden boat revival in the United States for two decades.

WHEN WE REALIZE THAT A BOAT IS simply something in which we can travel across water without getting wet (or drowned), we realize how many ways there are to achieve such a thing. And when we look at the boats in this book, we realize what a sophisticated thing this simple idea has become after ten thousand and more years of boatbuilding.

To begin at the beginning, with a nautical cliché, we envision a primitive man astride a log, paddling with his hands and crossing a stream to the wonder of his brethren ashore. It is certainly plausible that something such as this happened at the dawn of small-boat history, although an astute historian and naval architect has pointed out what an unstable vehicle a log can be, speculating that some of the first disastrous log trips may have set boat-building progress back hundreds of years. Ancient artwork shows Mesopotamian soldiers crossing water supported by inflated animal skins, East Indian women buoyed up by clay pots, a Cretan priestess afloat on a bundle of reeds—all examples of people using material that floats to float themselves. Something that floats begins to be a boat when it has been given some structure, much as a piece of flint becomes a tool when it is shaped into a handhold and an edge, and we may guess that this happened to boats more than one hundred centuries ago. Boat paddles dating back to 7500 B.C. have been found in Europe, and there is evidence of trade by water in the eastern Mediterranean ten thousand years ago—evidence in the form of stones from quarries far away that could only have arrived afloat.

Below, an old engraving depicts Spaniards and their gear aboard a balsa boat on Lake Titicaca in colonial days. The photo at right shows us a man in our own time aboard a lapstrake sailing canoe. The man seems to be having fun; the Spaniards are not. But both boats are simple, and similar in function going places on the water more or less efficiently.

© Northwind Picture Archives

© Neil Rabinowitz

The earliest boats were logs that had been hollowed out, an elaboration of the ancient man's vehicle; skins that had been stretched over a basketlike framework, an improvement on the animal-skin inflatable; and bundles of buoyant reeds wide in the middle and pointed at the ends where they were bound together. Examples of all three are still around—dugout canoes all over the world, reed boats on the lakes of East Africa and on Lake Titicaca in Bolivia and Peru, skin boats in Ireland and Wales and among the Eskimo.

THE FIRST WOODEN BOATS

Evidence suggests that building boats from pieces of wood began with the Egyptians, although dugouts with rough planks pegged or lashed on to build up the sides or added to the central hull in the form of outriggers are more ancient than we will ever know. In fact, we don't know that the Egyptians were the first true wooden-boat builders; we only know, because of the vast record they left, that boats were built of wood in Egypt as many as five thousand years ago. The common wooden boats of the Nile were made from acacia wood, which could be cut only in short pieces, and we have some record of how they were put together.

Here is a description of Egyptian boat building given to us by Herodotus in 450 B.C. (The old boy was not always a trustworthy historian, but here we have no reason for doubt): "They cut a quantity of planks about two cubits in length [about a yard or meter], and then begin their boat building, arranging the planks like bricks, and fixing them together with long spikes set close together until the hull is complete, when they lay cross pieces on top from side to side. They give the boat no ribs, and they caulk the seams with papyrus on the inside."

Herodotus noticed the most important feature of Egyptian boat building—firm fastenings

One of the simplest and most ancient of boat types is the reed boat, made by bundling buoyant reeds together. Here we see another representation of a boat from Lake Titicaca, a place where reed boats are still in use, as they are on the lakes of East Africa.

© Northwind Picture Archives

The Egyptian tomb painting below shows us a stylized version of a Nile River boat; although built of wood, its leaflike shape and delicacy imitate the reed boats that preceded it. At right is a representation of the bridge of boats allegedly built across the Hellespont by Xerxes of Persia. These boats are closer to Mediterranean types from the Middle Ages than to anything Xerxes might have used; but they show how the smooth-plank construction schemes of the Egyptians developed in the world of the later Mediterranean into husky, rounded boats for carrying cargo.

© Northwind Picture Archives

between planks. Because so many short lengths of wood had to be bound into a relatively water-tight shell with no ribs, the pieces had to be joined every which way, and this was done with mortise-and-tenon joints and with wooden dowels to pin the edges together. There were a lot of them. The boat that Herodotus describes was a small one and probably typical of the fleet on the Nile in his time and long before and after. But there were larger vessels. One of the largest we know about is a leaf-shaped ship 142 feet long (43 meters) and 19 feet wide (almost 6 meters) discovered adjacent to the pyramid of Cheops and dating to around 2500 B.C. Its 1,224 pieces represent several kinds of wood, including hop hornbeam from Asia Minor and local acacia and sycamore, but all the planking is Lebanese cedar in lengths as great as 72 feet (22 meters). Scarfs are made in the planks to join them end to end, and mortise-and-tenon joints align their edges.

Not a lot has changed in the building of wooden ships and boats in thousands of years. Boatwrights still hew hundreds of wooden parts into intricate and graceful shapes using hand tools and an artist's eye, although wooden vessels are now built from the inside out—ribs first, then planking. Here a boat carpenter works on the skeleton of Californian, *an interpretation of a nineteenth-century revenue vessel.*

41

At right is an artifact from the tomb of Tutankhamen—a model of an Egyptian ship from 3,300 years ago. The ship found in the tomb of Cheops was similar, but it was not a model. It was a real ship, the oldest yet discovered, and it was 142 feet (42.6 meters) long.

There is also an intricate system of rope lashings on the inside of the hull that literally stitches the planks to one another and sews them to sixteen frames inside. Across the top of the hull are forty-six deck beams that fasten into the uppermost planks. The Cheops ship is the oldest vessel artifact we have, and it may have been an old type in 2500 B.C.; Egyptian petroglyphs that show vessels similar to it date back five thousand years.

The ship of Cheops was a larger and more complicated version of the boat-building technology that Herodotus described 2,100 years later, and it made use of several methods of joining planks that would persist in boatbuilding to our own time—stitching wood together, common in India and the East, as well as fastening planks with mortise-and-tenon joints, a Mediterranean

method. Even the little boat described by Herodotus has a descendant today in strip-built hulls whose thin planks are edge-nailed much like the pegged-together boat of the Nile. By 2500 B.C. Egyptian boat builders used adzes, gravers, chisels, axes, mallets, planes, and even simple saws, and their work is something we can admire today in an age of power tools and fine cabinet-making. Egyptian boat builders were excellent craftsmen because they had to be—their boats had no internal framing to speak of (boats built from the inside out, with full skeletons to which planks were attached, did not come along until perhaps A.D. 1000). And the upswept ends of Egyptian boats, imitating the familiar and ancient reed boats of the Nile, made it all the more difficult to build a stable structure using many small pieces of wood.

Below and at right are details of an Adirondack guideboat built early in this century by W. A. Martin of Saranac Lake, New York. Although it looks ancient, it incorporates some new techniques in the building of small wooden boats, notably the ribs shown below, which were sawed from large spruce roots, and the fine edge-nailed deck planks at right.

INDIA AND THE EAST

Neil Hollander, an expert on Third World working vessels, described boats on the Indian sub-continent in 1980: "Many of the Bangladesh riverboats so closely resemble ancient Egyptian types that it seems as if they were built from drawings on the walls of the Pharaohs' temples.... This migration of ideas apparently occurred about 4000 years ago when Egyptian vessels sailed out of the Red Sea and discovered a wider world." The Bangladesh *pallar* he describes is leaf shaped and steers with a long oar fitted with a small lever for the helmsman's hand. A boat drawn on an ancient potsherd from the Indus valley has the same little lever on its oar/rudder. Authorities on nautical history before the Greeks agree that boat-building techniques in Egypt, Mesopotamia, and India are very similar, and they guess that contact among these civilizations—Indian-Arab-Mesopotamian contact in the Persian Gulf as well as Indian-Arab-Egyptian contact in the Red Sea—is the reason. There is not much historical record, but similar boats still exist from these places: boats of often similar shape and with firm edge-to-edge planking and an absence of strong interior framework; boats built of "a quantity of planks" and with a system of "arranging the planks like bricks." Today many of these boats, like the Bangladesh pallar, have plank-to-plank fastenings of iron nails or staples. Others are sewn together just like the ship of Cheops. Early Egyptian boats—dating from 3000 to 2500 B.C.—are thought to have been sewn together and given some mortise-and-tenon joints. The mortise-and-tenon method of fastening planks only became common in the middle Egyptian period—by 1800 B.C.—and sewing was slowly supplanted by carpentry methods thereafter.

Indian boats—as well as those of various Pacific islands, Sri Lanka, Indonesia, and other waterfronts of the East—are still sewn together with strong fibers rather than pinned together with mortises or dowels. The Arab vessels that dominated the Mediterranean in Crusader days had sewn planks, too. Why didn't these boat builders adopt the near-cabinetmaking methods of the Egyptian's in securing planks into a tight structure with wood joints and pegs? There are many possible reasons: They may not have had the bronze tools the Egyptians had, especially in more primitive places; they may have already had a strong, satisfactory tradition of literally sewing boats together—even large ones; and they may have found that boring little holes in planks and passing lashings through was easier and quicker. This last theory seems pretty convincing. Boats half a world away, in Scandinavia, in 1500 B.C. are thought to have had sewn planks, too; it was an obvious, simple way to make the structure tight.

We do not know how the stone-carrying vessels that plied the Mediterranean ten thousand years ago were put together. The post-Egyptian boats of the Mediterranean, however, carried on the Nile-River tradition of carefully fastened planks, smooth surfaces, and fine woodworking once they had evolved from the dugout-canoe stage. In the Aegean around 3000 B.C. most boats were small dugouts, although some of them were huge war canoes of 65 to 70 feet (20 to 21.5 meters) made from old-growth pine. It should be noted here that the Maori vessels of four thousand years later, the boats that settled New Zealand, were similar huge canoes of kauri pine, put together as catamarans with a substantial roofed house between the hulls.

All this is an indication that something Sir Walter Raleigh once said is worth remembering: "The truth is that all Nations how remote soever, being all reasonable creatures, and enjoying one and the same Imagination and Fantasie, have devised according to their means and materials the same things." Wooden boats are similar in many places around the world because they have to do the same things: to slice the water, they are pointed in front; to bear a load and

© Benjamin Mendlowitz

Built in Scotland by the renowned Fife yacht yard in 1931, for a military gentleman who planned a maiden voyage to the South Seas, the 107-foot (32-m) **Altair** *is one of the world's great schooner yachts. Since 1947 she has been based in the Mediterranean, always active during the summer season, and always cared for. In recent years, the Mediterranean's fleet of great old luxury yachts has grown significantly, the result of multi-million dollar restoration projects unique to Europe.*

Yachts under construction in a Pacific Northwest boatshop exemplify techniques that have been standard in western boatbuilding for several hundred years—an intricate skeleton of steam-bent wood on which skin planking will be fastened.

be stable, they are full and wide in the middle; and to float, they must be reasonably watertight. Their construction schemes may be similar because the "Imagination and Fantasie" of the boat builders or—perhaps more importantly the tools—are the same.

The first planked-up wooden boats were Egyptian, as far as we can tell, and they probably date back more than five thousand years. We have no small-boat remains from so long ago; but we have ship remains from 3,300 years ago, and we may guess that the boats of those times—vessels smaller than 40 feet (12 meters), say, and not meant to go to sea—were built much like the ships. A 50-foot (15-meter) Phoenician ship recently discovered off the Turkish coast, dating to the fourteenth century B.C., is made from fir planks fastened to one another and to what is thought to be

The woods used in a traditional yacht like this one have their standards, too—white oak for keel, ribs and other frame members, mahogany for trim, and often strips of teak on the decks.

a fir keel by mortise-and-tenon joints and with hardwood pegs. This is similar to Egyptian construction, and it is similar to the method Homer describes in his account of Odysseus building a little ship on Calypso's island.

By the late Egyptian period, wooden boats and ships were probably being built all around the eastern Mediterranean—and, we may guess, in India, Arabia, and Mesopotamia as well. Seafaring Canaanite (Phoenician) ships are shown in the Egyptian art of the fourteenth century B.C. delivering goods. The Phoenicians then were trading copper, tin, ivory, glass, weapons, pottery, gold, and silver all over the Mediterranean. The ship found in Turkey even had scrap gold and silver aboard—some of it from Egypt. And there were other seafarers. Mysterious raiders, known

Two boats from the Azores—a big fishing dragger below and a small fishing launch at right—show some workboat traditions of construction and finish: relatively bulky frames that are sawn rather than bent to shape, pine planking, and plain paint rather than varnish work.

to the Egyptians as the Sea Peoples, and thought to have sailed from the Aegean, ravaged the eastern Mediterranean in the twelfth and thirteenth centuries B.C. and were finally defeated by Rameses in the Nile Delta about 1174 B.C.. King Solomon had a fleet in the tenth century B.C. that he built and campaigned with Hiram, the Phoenician king of Tyre, in what is now Lebanon. In those ancient days Hiram and the Phoenicians and their Ships of Tarshish had a regular trade with far-away Spain in gold, silver, ivory, apes, and peacocks.

Ship building and boat building were flourishing in the Mediterranean by the time of Homer's *Odyssey*, and the method called "carvel"— the smooth skin of many planks fitted edge to edge and caulked with various materials for watertightness—became established from the Red Sea to the Adriatic. The Romans followed Greek and Phoenician boat-building practice, allegedly learning much of it from the Carthaginians. On one occasion a mostly intact Carthaginian galley came ashore on a Roman beach and taught them a lesson in ship building.

Whether the edge-to-edge, Egyptian-style planks of boats in the classical world were strengthened by much of a framework is still debated by scholars and archaeologists. Here are some of their opinions: "It seems probable that plank-and-frame construction had fully developed before ancient Greece rose to maritime prominence," wrote one. "For a period stretching from some time prior to 3000 B.C. until about A.D. 1500 boats had been built from the outside inwards. The shell planking was formed, the stiffening framework added afterwards," wrote another. Thucydides, the Greek historian who died circa 400 B.C., tells us that the keel-and-rib framework of boats was an invention of the Corinthians in the fifth century B.C. Modern historians of shipbuilding and boatbuilding claim evidence of "skeleton" construction—ribs first, then planking—in the eastern Mediterranean in about A.D. 1000; others find no evidence of plank-*on*-frame until the time of Columbus, the fifteenth century. And Basil Greenhill, former director of England's National Maritime Museum, wisely opined that there were "things in between" pure skeleton construction and the all-skin Egyptian boat that Herodotus tells us was built without ribs.

The Greek *triremes* launched in the time of Herodotus were mostly over 120 feet (36.5 meters) long, supported 170 or more oarsmen on three levels, stood the stresses of oar power and sailing rigs, carried some soldiers and archers on their upperworks, and were intended to ram and sink enemy ships. They certainly had structure, whether it was added after the planks were pinned together with mortise-and-tenon joints or was part of the building process. It is generally agreed that plank-*on*-frame construction was not established in wooden boat building and ship building until the late Middle Ages in Europe—but there was a buildup of structure from the time of the pharaohs until a frame-first, planking-afterward system became the way to build wooden ships and boats in Europe and America.

NORTHERN EUROPE

Meanwhile, in northern Europe, boats were being built in a different way (but with the same debates current about how much structure was inside the planking and whether it was there as a skeleton before the planks were hung). Northern European boats, variously described as wooden descendants of skin boats on wicker frames or elaborated dugouts, were made from thin, overlapped planks—a type of construction we have come to call "clinker," or "lapstrake." These boats were built like clapboard houses—such an obvious way to make a tight structure it is a wonder that other boat-building people didn't think of it.

The fresco from Thera in the Greek archipelago, at left, shows a rowing galley of a fine-lined Egyptian type. The chunky Mediterranean launch shown below looks very different, yet both of these boats are in the same tradition of smooth-skin planking and upswept ends tapering at bow and stern.

As a matter of fact, some of them did. On the Ganges and linking rivers of India and Pakistan, there is an ancient tradition of lapstrake boat building, from glorified dugouts to vessels of 50 feet (15 meters), and this is another reminder that Sir Walter Raleigh was a wise man (or, less likely, a suggestion that the Vikings visited India). Northern lapstrake boats date back to perhaps 2000 B.C. The earliest were probably sewn together, like so many other boats whose builders lacked metal fastenings and did not yet use pegs, or dowels, or treenails. The planks were lashed to one another with animal sinews or the thin roots or branches of shrubs. There were also raised "cleats" carved on the inside of the planks and sewn to frames that were ordinarily fashioned from the natural crooks of tree branches. In a very old boat discovered in a bog in England in 1938 and dated to between 900 and 700 B.C., the thick planks were not overlapped, but they had a rough tongue-and-groove connection and were sewn with yew, caulked with moss, and finished off with oak seam battens lashed in place on the inside of the hull. Other pieces, including a thick keel, were scarfed together into a tight structure, and the few ribs were fastened to cleats raised in the planks. This 40-foot (12-meter) boat looks like a dugout canoe made from pieces of wood, but it represents the beginnings of a type of boat building that, with metal fastenings, persists into our own time in the small boats of Scandinavia.

A much more sophisticated boat for a dozen or more paddlers is a 52-footer (almost 16 meters) dug up in Norway and dated to 350 to 300 B.C. Seven pieces of wood were sewn together with twisted gut—a flat keel piece, two overlapped planks on either side, and two gunwale planks. Inside were twenty ribs of hazel branches lashed to cleats raised in the thin pine planking. This one has the lightness and elegance of a modern lapstrake canoe, and its curved bifid (divided into two equal lobes) ends resemble drawings of boats in ancient Scandinavian scratchings

Modern sailing yachts designed in traditional style most often adopt the fine bow, bowsprit, and fancy trailboards that were features of the great clipper ships of the nineteenth century. The clippers were so much admired in their time that they gave these features to last-century yachts, steam launches, and even fishing boats. At left, with all the clipper details, is Kaiulani, a schooner yacht built in the 1980s in California. Her wheel, below, is another traditional touch, the same wheel that Nova Scotia's Lunenburg Foundry has supplied to ships and yachts for more than a hundred years.

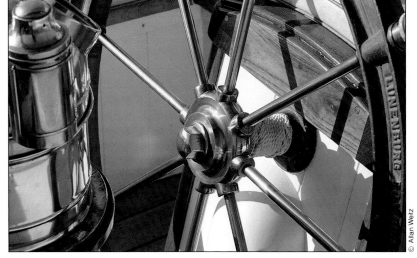

Another recent example of the clipper style is Whitehawk, one of the most spectacular sailing yachts built in recent decades. A perfect blend of modern and traditional, she carries up-to-the-minute sailing and mechanical gear, and her hull is cold-molded wood—a new form of construction that uses veneers of wood fastened with epoxy adhesive.

© Dan Nerney

© Neil Rabinowitz

on rock. A 76-foot (23-meter) rowing galley found in northern Germany and dated to around A.D. 400 had five lapped planks per side and a flat keel piece. Plank fastening consisted of rows of iron nails clenched over little washers that modern lapstrake boatbuilders call "roves." There were nineteen ribs of grown-oak (natural-limb) crooks, and these were lashed to cleats raised in the planks. A 90-foot (27-meter) Saxon ship found in England and dated to A.D. 600 had 1-inch- (2.5-centimeter-) thick planks thought to be of oak (the archaeologists found only the lovely impression of the vessel in the sand of a burial mound and so couldn't name the wood) and strengthened by twenty-six heavy frames about 3 (.9 meter) feet apart. Fastenings were iron bolts and spikes and hundreds of iron rivets.

The Viking boat building of one thousand years ago is the legacy—and perhaps the pinnacle—of these northern lapstrake traditions. The Oseberg ship of A.D. 800, a 68-foot (almost 21-meter) rowing-sailing vessel found in the burial mound of a Viking queen, is such an exquisite example of boat carpentry it can hardly be described. Here is one description from the historian and boat designer Phil Bolger:

> The discipline lay in arranging the timbers in such a way that no two should be rigidly joined cross-grain. The mass of wood must be free to shrink in the boathouse and swell in the sea without stressing either the fastenings or the grain. The grown frames lay cross-grain to the planking, but the connection was in resilient lashings. Natural-crook planking swept up at the ends to land on the rabbets with grain almost tangent to that of the stem and stern posts. The rules of the boatbuilder's craft gave optimum size and shape for all components, all to be hewn with axe and adze since no self-respecting craftsman would tear up the grain with a saw even if he had seen one in the decadent South.

The Oseberg ship is an extraordinary wooden sculpture, decorated with jewellike carvings and

Fisherman-style schooners, based on the big vessels that harvested the North Atlantic from the 1890s into the 1950s, represent another traditional type of sailing yacht. Above is Phra Lwang, a racing-cruising schooner designed by the legendary John Alden.

Before the clipper yachts, and even before the big clipper ships, there were fast clipper schooners built in Baltimore in the 1830s and 1840s. They gave their rakish style and fine lines to the ships and smaller vessels that came later. Californian, *shown here, is a new vessel with Baltimore Clipper lines and rig, an interpretation of the United States Revenue Service vessel* Joe Lane *of 1849.*

sweeping in sweet curves from end to end and upward in stem and stern posts that curl into a fine spiral. And its descendants, the lapstrake boats of our own century, keep the same lightness and integrity and elegance of line.

One other tradition of early boatbuilding deserves mention—the flat-section barge. When Julius Caesar sailed to Britain in 55 B.C., he saw Celtic ships that he admired for their ruggedness. In his account of the conquest of Gaul he writes:

> Their ships were built and rigged in this manner: the hulls were somewhat flatter than those of our ships, so that they were more suitable for the shallows and the ebbing of the tide. The bows were rather upright, and they and the sterns were suited to the great size of the stormy seas. The ships were built entirely of oak, so as to stand any shock. The cross timbers were made of beams a foot thick fastened with iron nails as thick as a thumb. The anchors were fitted with iron chains instead of ropes. The sails were of skins and thin leather, either for lack of flax and ignorance of its use or, as seems more likely, because canvas sails were not considered able to support such force of wind and drive such heavy vessels.

These tough ships of broad planks, relatively flat surfaces, and iron fastenings had something in common with the *junks* and *sampans* (flat-bottomed skiffs) of the Chinese—a massive conception of shipbuilding using heavy timbers and bulkheads for internal structure. The remains of smaller vessels like them have been found in the Thames at London and elsewhere in Europe, and there are similar rough-hewn boats made with wide boards and angular frames here and there around the world. Among these flat-bottomed boats—including scows, bateaus, punts, and barges—are some graceful types, such as the Venetian gondola and the dories of North America. The flat-floored fishing *pinnaces* of the Bay of Biscay, located between France and Spain;

When the Angles and Saxons, and a bit later the Vikings, invaded the British Isles, they brought their Baltic and North Sea boat-building traditions with them. The Thames River rowing skiff shown here, with its hornlike rowlocks, lapstrake planking, and distinctive curve of bow, is a near relation to small boats found in Viking burial mounds.

the fishing scows of France's Loire River; the huge houseboats of India's Kashmir; the River Thames barges of London; and even the recreational punts of English rivers are all variations on the obvious idea of making a necessarily flat-section boat from broad planks. Discussing small boats of this type, John Gardner tells us in *The Dory Book*, "Some authorities think that double-ended, flat-bottom boats at one time had a range from Egypt to Denmark," and he traces the ancestry of the New England dory back to the *battoes* of the French fur traders, a type that was known in the Middle Ages in Europe and may even have descended from the small boats of the Gauls.

Refinements of all these types have come along in the last thousand years, along with some new boat-building techniques. So-called skeleton construction—framework first, then planking—is now the method used in building round-section boats of various ancestry, from Australian yachts to Portuguese workboats. Thin, steam-bent ribs, first applied in the eighteenth century in Europe, have replaced tree-branch crooks in the framework of lightweight boats, which range from wooden canoes to sportfishing powerboats. And strong, waterproof glues have made it possible to build one-piece boats from thin sheets or strips of wood.

The wooden boats of our time represent nearly all the traditions and technologies of the past. The workboats of the Mediterranean world, from Greek and Turkish *caïques* to diesel fishing boats in Portugal, have the same smooth planking, caulked seams, and thick ribs that characterized Phoenician trading ships and Roman galleys. The small coastal boats of northern Europe, from British yacht tenders to Norwegian and Polish fishing vessels, have the lapped, riveted planks and upswept ends of the Viking ships. The wide-board boats, from dories to gondolas to Chesapeake Bay workboats, represent the same idea, if not the same ancestry, as the Celtic boats dug out of the mud of the Thames by nautical archaeologists.

The wooden boats in this book represent most of the old methods of putting wood together to make a boat, and today's wooden-boat-building shops, disdaining fiberglass (but not epoxy adhesive), are busy putting boats together using most of the old traditions. The boats they like to build tend to be nineteenth-century models, because plans and records of traditional boats from the last century are available and because the nineteenth century's combination of metal

At left, Leo Telesmanick of the Concordia boatyard in South Dartmouth, Massachusetts, builds a new Beetle Cat. Leo has been hand-crafting these boats since the 1930s, and his shop is one of hundreds still building classic wooden boats with traditional tools and materials.

technology (good, cheap tools and fastenings), available wood (the forests of North America), and organization of craftsmanship (boat shops of many men working as teams and essentially as trade schools) produced what are perhaps the best wooden boats of a ten-thousand-year history.

WOODEN-BOAT BUILDING TODAY

In the late 1970s, when the wooden-boat revival was building up steam, a writer, scholar, zealot and adventurer named Paul Lipke went on a pilgrimage to every shop in North America he could discover that might be still building plank-on-frame boats. He traveled 40,000 miles (64,360 kilometers) during eighteen months, and he visited 3,000 boatyards from British Columbia to

This pretty overnight-cruising sloop was designed in the 1920s, and boats like her have yet to be surpassed for style and performance. And thanks to the wooden-boat revival, boats like her are still produced by small shops that carry on the best traditions of yachtbuilding in wood.

Louisiana to Michigan and Maine. There were, he says, "about 600 at that time" still building wooden boats, and he focused on 150 of them as significant wooden-boat shops. Lipke produced a book titled *Plank on Frame*, published in 1980 by International Marine Publishing of Camden, Maine, and it remains the most complete reference to wooden-boat building in North America. Since the book was written, some of these shops—many of them one-man or one-woman enterprises—may have closed their doors. Other shops will have opened, so keep this in mind as you are using it. The best source of information about builders of wooden boats, updated every sixty days, is *WoodenBoat* magazine, which fills its back pages with advertisements from builders of everything from lapstrake skiffs to classic sailing yachts.

But wouldn't these small shops, their boats handcrafted, built in small (often single) production sequences, necessarily produce boats that are more expensive than boats made from fiberglass or riveted aluminum? A good question, and what follows is something of an answer. A rough survey of builders of various types of wooden boats and a comparison of their prices with those of similar products manufactured in fiberglass show that wooden boats are surprisingly competitive despite the labor-intensive nature of wooden-boat building and the alleged production economies of boat manufacturing in plastic. Elite wooden boats made from the finest grades of oak, cedar, mahogany, and teak and with fit and finish of cabinetmaking quality are as much as three times more expensive than plainer examples of the same type in fiberglass. But workboat types—simple rowing and sailing skiffs; wooden lobster-boat and lapstrake sea-skiff hulls finished off as cruisers; and traditional sailing yachts or yacht-style working boats without expensive finishing or rigging details—can be built in wood for less than the cost of their fiberglass sisters. Some types of boats—diesel cruisers, small day sailers, family-size sailing auxiliaries—seem to be about the same price with similar accommodations and equipment, whether they are made of wood or fiberglass. And wooden speedboats that are replicas of mahogany runabouts from the 1920s and 1930s are often cheaper than fiberglass performance boats of similar size and power. Yes, varnished mahogany runabouts and fiberglass deep-vee sports boats are like apples and oranges, and comparisons are difficult (and odious). But the prices of hand-built wooden boats of various types and sizes and the prices of manufactured boats that do the same things are often comparable. This may have to do with the lean lifestyles of wooden-boat builders and the fact that a fiberglass boat—put together in an expensively tooled factory, advertised in magazines and at boat shows, and sold to dealers who take their cut before they make a deal with you—carries what we may kindly call "hidden costs."

Is owning a wooden boat worthwhile? Most owners of wooden boats seem to think so. They are not thinking of over ten thousand years of history. They are not thinking of the prices of their boats as compared with the prices of the major boating appliances owned by their neighbors. They are not thinking (we hope) of the many hours of maintenance and refinishing their boats may demand. They are thinking the same thoughts we all think when we look at the boats in this book—how lovely, how appropriate, how clever, how interestingly shaped this boat is. Whether they recognize it or not, they are thinking of beauty and truth.

ROWING AND PADDLING BOATS

Some wooden boats are
elegant for the beauty of
their finish, painted or
varnished; others are
elegant for the way the
wood bends and sweeps
into a whole that seems
predestined. Some are
distinguished by their
delicacy, others by their
ruggedness. All are classic
for the way their forms
derive from their
functions.

Traditional rowing boats are shown on the previous page, and at opposite. The Adirondack guideboat shown on pages 64-65, meant to be rowed effortlessly for hours by fishing guides on placid lakes, is fine-lined and lightweight. The collection of boats—which includes a cedar canoe, a peapod, and several flatiron skiffs—is part of the fleet of Seattle's Center for Wooden Boats.

BOATS FOR ROWING AND PADDLING HAVE ALL THE VIRTUES OF SIMPLICITY. They are more affordable than other types of boats. They are easy to care for during the boating season and easy to stow away at home during the winter. The light ones can be carried from one interesting waterway to another on a cartop or a boat trailer. The instant recreation they make possible is just as simple and satisfying as their physical attributes. No messing with engines and their sometimes fussy behavior. No expense for fuel (you provide it yourself with the fat you've built up over the winter). No spending half an hour rigging or otherwise preparing the boat before getting started. Rowing and paddling boats represent not only freedom from fuss, but also—like all boats (and maybe a little more than like other boats)—they offer an instant escape from the care and clamor of the shore.

In a recent essay in *Nautical Quarterly*, wooden-boat writer Peter Spectre wrote about the dead-simple painted rowboat that he keeps year-round down at the harbor in the town where he lives. The essay took him back thirty years to his first time in a rowboat as a boy: "Freedom is what rowboats have represented to me since that day. The ability to walk down the road to the harbor or the shore and step into a little boat without any preparation whatsoever, sit down on the thwart, slide the oarlocks into the sockets, cast off the painter, put the oars into the oarlocks, take a long pull and be free."

The Adirondack guideboat below, and the modern recreational rowing shell at right, have about the same dimensions and weight. A race between them would be close. The guideboat is built lapstrake using sawed ribs of cedar.

The Appledore Pod from Martin Marine in Kittery Point, Maine, is made in one piece from cold-molded sheets of western red cedar.

© Allan Weitz

© Allan Weitz

FORM FOLLOWS FUNCTION

Rowing and paddling boats are often elegant things—and if, like Peter Spectre's plain skiff, they may lack the élan of, say, Adirondack guideboats or college shells, they at least have the virtue of honesty, of something that does its job unpretentiously and well. Most of the rowing and paddling boats in this book have that elegance; all of them have that honesty. When Louis Sullivan said that form follows function, he was talking about the large buildings he created. His comment became a tenet of twentieth-century design, but the tenet fits everything from nature's design for birds to man's design for a better mousetrap. It fits rowing and paddling boats especially well. Some of them are elegant for the beauty of their finish, painted or varnished; others are elegant for the way the wood bends and sweeps into a whole that seems predestined (in fact, the shapes of many kinds of boats are determined by the way their wood bends). Some of them, like college shells and cedar canoes, are elegant for their delicacy; others, like Maine peapods and Jersey-shore surfboats, are distinguished by their ruggedness. All are classic for the way their forms derive from their functions.

The forms of all rowing and paddling boats follow to a greater or lesser extent their functions as human-powered machines. The fastest and most efficient of them all, the eights rowed by college athletes, are typically 58 feet (17.5 meters) long and 2 feet (.6 meter) wide and weigh around 200 pounds (90 kilograms). The first Oxford eight of 1829 was 45 feet (almost 14 meters) long and 4 feet, 3 inches (1.2 meters) wide and weighed 2,434 pounds (about 1 metric ton). A few things have improved in 160 years, notably lightweight construction techniques, but the principles that make for the fastest single-hull boats remain the same: great waterline length, narrow beam, and lightest possible weight. In commenting on the Oxford eight of 1829—and following up discus-

Reflecting her crisp lapstrake lines in still water, this Jersey skiff was built a dozen years ago at Maine's Apprenticeshop. Less-fancy boats like her served fishermen and lifesaving services on the Jersey coast one-hundred years ago, and are still used by beach life guards.

sions of the Gokstad Viking ship, the Venetian gondola, and the Eskimo kayak—the great English yacht designer Uffa Fox wrote in *Seamanlike Sense in Powercraft:*

> The lines are long and easy as one would expect from a boat which has a length of over ten times her beam. So, once again, we see that in Norway, Italy, Greenland and England the development of the most easily driven vessel is exactly the same; all have great length to keep wave-making down to the minimum, narrow beam to keep the weight and surface friction to the minimum—the two things that control the speed of a displacement boat.

He might have added that the same principles apply to modern destroyers, among the fastest of naval ships, and to ocean liners, whose speed is not only a result of their engine power, but also of extreme waterline lengths, which move them along despite their bulk.

Some of the rowing and paddling boats in this book are long, slim, and light; others have compromised one thing or another for ruggedness or stability or the need to carry a load. And some in their original forms have sacrificed length because they didn't need it. Length means weight; length means more structure inside; length means planks longer than the builder may have been able to get out of local forest resources, as happened to the Egyptians.

Canoes and kayaks of all kinds are light and not especially long because one or two people have to be able to lift them to load them onto a cartop, to bring them ashore, and to portage through the woods. Peapods and Banks dories are beamy and built without considerations of weight or delicacy because they were originally workboats that got knocked around a lot and because beam gave them stability and load-carrying capacity. Peapods were originally used for inshore fishing on the Maine coast, with one man aboard hauling lobster traps or spearing eels. Banks dories were developed for trawl fisheries far offshore, in which dories with two men and their gear aboard would

Two local classics shown here are the Adirondack guideboat at left and the lapstrake Whitehall boat below. Adirondack guideboats, like their cousins the St. Lawrence skiffs, were built by the thousands to serve summer cottages and resort hotels. Whitehall boats, named for Manhattan's Whitehall Street, were utility boats in the Port of New York in clipper-ship days. This one has the slim lines and lapstrake planking of the earliest Whitehalls, with the modern addition of a sliding seat.

71

Part of the wooden-boat revival in England is Constable's Boathouse at Hampton on the Thames, and its proprietor, Mark Edwards, shown at right with one of his venerable boats. Constable's rents and repairs River Thames skiffs, and part of the equipage of a rental is the tin of tallow for the oarlocks shown below.

be dropped from fishing schooners to set and retrieve baited trawls and return with a load of fish that would just about sink the boat. Banks dories, with their flaring sides, become more stable as weight sinks them down. Jersey-shore beach boats—used in the last century for fisheries that operated off the sand and now in the service of lifeguards—are designed with box-section keels and small, flat bottoms, full and flaring topsides, and upswept ends, to be rushed into the surf and rowed off the beach with good tracking and stability and with enough oar power to be able to breast the first two or three waves of surf into calmer water. All of these boats are specialized, even though immutable principles of weight, length, and shape determine how easily they can be paddled or rowed.

A detail view of one of the Constable's Boathouse skiffs shows an intricately made floorboard grating. Most of the boats that Mark Edwards rents for excursions on the Thames are more than a hundred years old.

73

Two basic rowing boats—one simple and one sophisticated—are shown here. The 6 foot, 5-inch (2-m) Tortoise, at bottom, designed by Phil Bolger for homebuilding in plywood, is about as basic as a boat can get. The 13-foot (4-m) Marblehead dory skiff at right, designed by John Gardner based on dory builder William Chamberlain's legendary boats, is shapely and very capable. ''For a rowing sea boat, you can't do much better within the 13-foot (4-m) limit,'' Gardner says.

© Allan Weitz

© Allan Weitz

HISTORY

Rowing and paddling boats have an ancient history, from the primitive man's log to the Viking ships, but the traditional rowing and paddling types we see in these pages, and most other rowing and paddling boats in Europe, America, and Australia took their form in the nineteenth century. Their construction methods were very old—the first Oxford eight was a lapstrake boat like the Viking ships, a method of boat building favored in our own day by builders in Britain and Scandinavia and certain places in the United States—but their refined shapes, wise details, and sheer perfection seem to have appeared suddenly in the last century.

Suddenly is not too dramatic a word to describe the quick evolution of the many wonderful small boats of the nineteenth century, from recreational canoes to dories to Whitehall boats. The bulky ships' boats of the eighteenth century, the bateaus of the lumbermen, the sailing and rowing barges of the Dutch, and the heavy, Viking-derived fishing boats of the Scots and the Scandinavians seem to be no ancestors of the many varieties of small boats that came along in the last century, especially in America. There were ancestors, of course, but a combination of factors—the Industrial Revolution's cheap tools and fastenings, great resources of lumber, a boom in fishing and shipping, certainly more freedom and resourcefulness among boat builders competing with one another—caused the creation or rapid evolution of small-wooden-boat types that remain standards today, from the Oxford eight of 1829, grandfather of the college shell, to the Indian birchbark canoe that became the kind of upswept-end canoe, in wood or now in aluminum or fiberglass, that we identify today as "a canoe." One more reason for the persistence and popularity of these boats—and something we might call the "Egyptian factor"—is that we have much more evidence of nineteenth-century small-boat types than we have of boats from earlier times, evidence com-

Dories are simple, rugged boats made from wide planks on sawn frames. The classic dory is the Banks model shown here, named for the North Atlantic fishing banks where schooners carried dories and their men to fish with baited trawls. Banks dories were designed to nest like this on the decks of the big schooners.

© Allan Weitz

piled in this century by zealots such as the late Howard Chapelle of the Smithsonian Institution and John Gardner of Mystic Seaport.

Boats such as dories, Whitehalls, skiffs, and peapods were working boats in the last century. Today they are recreational boats for fishing, exercise, and just knocking around. As Peter Spectre testifies, they are also popular for the curious freedom they deliver without fail. Nearly all of them may be sailed as well as rowed or paddled, and a few of them appear under sail in this book. Some others we see in these pages are pure rowing or paddling boats, and a few are sliding-seat exercise machines designed in the past few decades with fitness in mind. All of them, in fact, can be vehicles for fitness—perhaps as much for tuning down the mental machinery as raising heart and respiration rates. Gliding along close to the water in a canoe and hearing only the sound of your paddle breaking the surface, taking a long morning pull around the harbor in a rowing skiff to see what boats have come in during the night, spending the hours before dark drifting in a small boat and casting for fish plucking the surface all around you—these are the simple and soul-satisfying experiences that rowing and paddling boats make possible. You can do these things in aluminum canoes and fiberglass dinghies, of course, but small wooden boats seem better choices. Their looks and materials suit the mood and the environment. They are as aesthetically pleasing as the passing shoreline, the sun lighting the water, the fine wake slipping away astern.

© Neil Rabinowitz

SAILBOATS

Wooden boats and sails are natural partners. Sails are an invention as old as wheels, and the first boats with sails are thought to have appeared more than five thousand years ago.

A Scandinavian heritage is evident in the crisp lines and lapstrake planking of the Folkboat on the previous pages. At opposite is Californian, *another evocation of heritage. Launched in 1984, she's the state of California's Tall Ship, an interpretation by Melbourne Smith of the United States Revenue Service vessels that patrolled the West Coast during the Gold Rush.*

EVERY CATEGORY OF WOODEN BOAT DISCUSSED IN THIS BOOK, except for speedboats, includes boats that sail: sailing canoes and rowing boats rigged with spritsails, luxury yachts built for big-time racing or to take you to the South Seas, even a few workboats. But the majority of wooden sailboats, in these pages and in our experience, are designed and built for pleasure—some for racing, some for cruising, some for daysailing and just knocking around. There are now about four hundred classes of sailboats in organized racing throughout the world, and nearly all of them built before 1960 were made of wood. Some of them still are.

And at any given time in recent years, there have been perhaps five thousand cruising sailboats roaming the oceans, some of them on circumnavigations that take three or four years. There are also cruising sailboats used for vacation voyages along the coasts and day sailers taken out for an evening ride around the harbor. Nearly every one of these boats was made of wood until fiberglass came along and brought huge increases in the numbers of sailboats and sailors during the sixties and seventies. Today, in marinas full of fiberglass sailboats with aluminum spars, a wooden sailboat is a rarity.

HISTORY

But wooden boats and sails are natural partners. Sails are an invention as old as wheels, and the first boats with sails are thought to have appeared more than five thousand years ago—perhaps

Two very different wooden yachts with similar rigs are shown here. The big cruising yacht flying a balloon spinnaker is a yawl—with her after mast all the way aft. The Rushton sailing canoe below is ketch-rigged—with her after mast forward of the rudder.

© Neil Rabinowitz

© Benjamin Mendlowitz

Egyptian reed boats on the Nile, perhaps skin boats fitted with crude sails in Mesopotamia. The Egyptians, Greeks, Phoenicians, Arabs, Persians, and Romans were early sailors. The Celtic ships of Julius Caesar's time sailed from what is now the French mainland to England and Ireland. In the Old English epic *Beowulf* of 1,500 years ago, the eponymous character and his company sailed to the land of the Danes. The Chinese were sailing huge vessels with four to six masts and crews of 150 to 300 in Marco Polo's time.

Sail is an ancient technology and, despite simple appearances, a complicated one. The power of wind is great enough to move very heavy objects at a good clip through the water, and it is great enough to require tough structure and sophisticated engineering in hulls, spars, fittings, and rigging. Paul Lipke, the man who investigated contemporary wooden-boat building in *Plank on Frame*, says that, "In general, ships represent the most sophisticated technology of any of the societies that have produced them—an unbroken chain of technology that was not surpassed until the age of flight." He's talking about wooden sailing ships and, by inference, wooden sailing boats.

TECHNOLOGY

Sailing ships and sailing boats are subject to greater stresses than other types of vessels. The mast can easily fall down and needs to be held up by firm structure at its base, called the "mast step," and by lines of steel cable, steel rod, or strong rope that guy (reinforce) the mast or masts to critical points of the hull, called the "shrouds" and "stays." The mast is especially prone to falling down or breaking when the power of wind fills the sails. And when the rigging is tuned like a violin string, the downward pressure could push the mast through the bottom of the boat or

Of all traditional sailboats, the catboat may be
the most beloved. Distinguished by its broad
beam, roominess, and big single sail, it has
been a favorite New England type for more
than 100 years. At right is a Beetle Cat, still
built in wood by the Concordia Company.
Below is a cruising cat built recently by the
Crosbys of Osterville, Massachusetts, to
a 1900 Crosby design.

84

One of the most capable seagoing boats of all time is the Bristol Channel pilot cutter, designed and built to deliver pilots to incoming ships in all weather on the stormy coast of England's West Country. Hirta, *shown at left, was built in 1911. A world-voyaging yacht today, she's been to the Greenland ice, to Russia, to the United States, and to the Caribbean in her travels.*

bend up the ends of the hull. Sailing ships and sailing boats are engineered to keep all these things from happening—fittings are made from strong stuff like bronze or stainless steel; wooden spars are straight-grained Sitka spruce with a critical amount of flexibility; hulls have strong backbones and extra strength built in where the stays and shrouds are attached; sails are the weakest link and tend to tear or even blow out before the rig suffers damage in a high wind and sea.

The sophisticated technology that Paul Lipke praises is exactly that—complex, clever, an evolution of engineering wisdom over five thousand years—but always vulnerable. As British (Ukrainian-born) novelist Joseph Conrad wrote of the British clipper ships he commanded, "What is the array of the strongest ropes, the tallest spars, and the stoutest canvas against the mighty breath of the infinite but thistle stalks, cobwebs, and gossamer?"

Small sailboats do not challenge the mighty breath of the infinite the way the sailing ships of the last century did, but they represent the same technology in miniature. And the seagoing sailboats of our time, some of them as small as 25 feet (7.5 meters) on deck, are all the more sophisticated for the David-versus-Goliath game they play with the world's oceans.

Most seagoing sailboats, and many classes of inshore racing boats (keelboats), have deep keels weighted with lead, sometimes tons of it. This counterweight opposes the force of wind on the sails and keeps the boat upright when the wind is on the beam. And the broad area of such a keel opposes the force of wind pushing the boat sideways. It also softens motion in steep chop or a high sea and stabilizes the whole apparatus when a sailboat is slicing into the wind, its sails functioning as airfoils, or when running with the breeze behind with the sails winged out to catch as much wind as possible. Deep weighted keels make it possible for relatively small sailboats to cross oceans. In a high wind and sea, with a small storm sail set to keep the boat's nose into the wind, a deep-keeled sailboat sits like a buoy, its crew below decks waiting for things to calm down. A powerboat can't do this and must plug along with the crew steering as best they can in wild conditions and praying that the engines don't quit. Only the largest power yachts cross oceans. Smaller and lighter sailboats that don't go to sea normally use centerboards, or daggerboards—plates that can be raised or lowered in a case through a slot in the boat's bottom—to counter the sideward push of wind on the sails, and they use crew weight on the windward side to counteract the force of wind in the sails that wants to tip the boat over.

Sailboats are specialized, strong, and a little bit complicated compared with other types of small boats. They are also beautiful and imbued with romance. A 12-meter designed and built to perfec-

© Allan Weitz

Sailboats of all kinds are constructed and equipped to accommodate the considerable stresses of wind and water. On a traditional sailboat, gear such as the wooden mast hoops, heavy boom-to-mast hardware, and plain rope shown above may be old-fashioned but they represent excellent engineering perfected over centuries.

Views of two Friendship sloops show a businesslike foredeck at left and a boat under sail in Penobscot Bay below. Developed in the last half of the nineteenth century for lobstering on the Maine coast, and named for Friendship, Maine, the town where the most famous builders of these boats set up shop, this clipper-style workboat is now a favorite traditional yacht.

That classic wooden sailboats are beautiful can't be denied. Here are two perfect examples—a Nordic Folkboat, a worldwide class of 26-foot (8-m) boats capable of everything from day-racing to crossing oceans, at right, and the little daysailing Beetle catboat shown below.

tion to race for the America's Cup or a modern, cold-molded wooden trimaran intended to race across the Atlantic have the spare, logical beauty of an aircraft or a racing car. A replica sailing ship and a cruising schooner share the beauty of traditional hull lines and rig and the romance of something that constitutes a little world of its own, at once a vehicle and a domicile, at home in port or ranging the wide world. Even a day-sailing dinghy has the beauty of a traditional small-boat hull and offers the simple satisfaction of managing its small sail and its lines with the sailor's two hands and intelligence. The romance is built in even on this small scale, especially on a summer day when the wind fills the sail, the hull slips along with a burble of water, and the sheet and the tiller vibrate in the helmsman's hands with the power of wind and water.

The beauty and romance of sailing are bound up with that controlled power. Sailors love sailing because their vehicles are so nicely arranged to use natural forces to advantage, and at the end of all the structure and engineering it is the sailor who manipulates the vessel and its sails, the wind and the water, the course and the goal—whether the course and the goal are a long gamble to win a race or a downwind slide to get from Los Angeles to Hawaii. Sailors love sailing for the seeming simplicity of the thing itself and for the complicated, challenging qualities of structure and rig, skills and judgment—indeed beauty and truth—that sailing vessels and sailing represent.

The wooden sailboats on these pages range from simple boats with simple sails to vessels capable of voyaging around the world. Most of them were designed and built for pleasure sailing, and part of the pleasure is the wood they're made from—teak decks, varnished mahogany trim, bright spruce spars, surfaces on deck and below worked and fitted in intricate and pleasing shapes. Other sailboats may be made from other stuff, and fiberglass, steel, and aluminum have their place; but wood is wonderful, as traditional-boat purists like to say. Wooden sailboats are the real thing. They have the style and substance of their ancestors, the wooden sailing workboats and yachts that defined for generations what the best of wooden-boat building could be.

WORKBOATS

Wooden workboats are artifacts not only of their particular types but of all wooden boats, in a family tree that goes back to the sailing barges the Dutch turned into yachts, to the lighters that provisioned the ships of Columbus, to the Saxon galleys that brought new settlers to England, to the boat the apostles used to fish the Sea of Galilee, to Charon the ferryman.

Beautiful in a different way from yachts and traditional rowing boats, workboats are plain-finished, ruggedly built, and all business. On the previous page is a Maine lobsterboat, and at opposite is a New England dragger. Both of these boats are old and made of wood; newer lobster boats are mostly fiberglass, and most other new fishing vessels are steel.

BEFORE 1800, NEARLY ALL WORKBOATS WERE WOOD and nearly all wooden boats were workboats. Workboats are the original wooden boats, and they represent every type and size, from the canoes of the French fur traders, to the Whitehall boats of the last century's New York Harbor merchants, to the big wooden schooners that fished the North Atlantic in this century. Wooden workboats survive all over the world, although in the United States and Europe the newer working vessels tend to be steel and sometimes aluminum or fiberglass.

CLASSIC WORKBOATS

Workboats even inspired the first yachts, which were luxury versions of familiar waterfront types— pilot boats, lighters, coastal traders. The little boats that gentlemen and ladies rowed on England's Thames and Cam rivers were much like the boats of the local ferrymen and fishermen. The relationship between boats that work and boats that play is still very close; the latter are often only refined versions of the former.

Some enduring wooden-workboat types in the United States and Canada are the Chesapeake Bay models that harvest crabs and oysters; Chesapeake Bay skipjacks that still drag the oyster beds under sail; many of the salmon gillnetters in the Pacific Northwest and Alaska; a few of the older boats in the shrimp and menhaden fleets of the South and in the various fishing fleets of New

© Jim Brown

Last of the wooden-workboat fleets in the United States, the skipjacks of Chesapeake Bay, shown here, still dredge for oysters under sail. Their owners work this old-fashioned way not by choice but under a law designed to keep the fleet in business and to conserve oyster beds that would be devastated by more efficient fishing.

England; and the lobster boats of New England and Canada, often still built of wood in Nova Scotia (although few new lobster boats are built of wood in Maine).

Meanwhile, in parts of the world where there are flourishing wooden-workboat yards and where metal and fiberglass hulls are either unknown or too expensive, workboats made of wood are not merely common—they are the only boats of any kind on the waterfront. It has been estimated that there are more wooden boats in Bangladesh, from dugouts to passenger ferries, than in all other nations of the world combined. The entire fishing and lighter fleet of Belize in Central America not only is made of wood but operates under sail. Indonesian lumber schooners and Chilean sloops in the firewood trade are made of wood and also carry wood as cargo. Dugouts, outriggers, and

One of the handsomest workboats in the world
is the New England sardine carrier, long and
slim and nearly all deck and hold space. These
boats take in tons of little fish that are hoisted
aboard in nets set by smaller vessels, and then
deliver the catch to processing plants.

wooden rafts are used for fishing all over the Pacific and on the coast of Brazil. Wooden boats with

gasoline or diesel engines, roughly comparable to *The African Queen*, still carry people and goods

on the rivers of Africa and South America.

FUNCTIONAL BEAUTY

Workboats are not yachts (although, as noted, some yachts look just like workboats). Boats that

service ships, catch fish, drag for scallops or oysters, carry cargo, or run waterfront errands get

knocked around a lot. Their finish is paint rather than varnish; their lines and on-deck structures

are simple rather than complex because they are working vessels owned by working men and

© Allan Weitz

Classic symbols of the Maine coast are lobsterboats like the one at right and lobster traps like those below. Peapods and Friendship sloops and several kinds of gas-engine launches harvested lobsters before 1920—but in the twenties the lobster boat evolved as the principal vessel in the fishery.

© Allan Weitz

women and they cannot be overly expensive; their construction tends to be heavy and extremely practical compared with their cousins in the yachting fleet. They have a style all their own, and it is the original style of all wooden boats, hard to improve upon even in yacht versions. It is the subtle, unstylish style that pickup trucks and Land Rovers have in the world of automobiles— plain, businesslike, oddly attractive.

A characteristic of workboats, as opposed to yachts, is that there is obvious space and accommodation for the kind of work they do. Sardine carriers are mostly hold space for the tons of little fish that come aboard from the smaller boats that net them or trap the fish in coves; the engine and pilothouse occupy only a small space aft. Skipjacks have deck space for sorting out oysters and handling sails; their cabins offer shelter from weather and a relatively clean place for the crew to gather for lunch. Lobster boats have similar accommodations for shelter, but are half working space; like all fishing boats, they are low-sided at some point—in this case aft—to make it easier to bring the catch aboard. Small tugboats and boatyard workboats are chunky and muscular with a tremendous amount of their space taken up by their engines; they are nautical locomotives whose big jobs—and big engines for their size—involve pushing-and-pulling power. Even peapods and sharpies are more capacious than they would have been if their original purposes were recreational.

Workboats are strictly business, and even those now made from metal or plastic owe their distinctive shapes and plain styles to the wooden boats that were their recent ancestors. The wooden workboats that survive are artifacts not only of their particular types but of all wooden boats, in a family tree that goes back to the sailing barges the Dutch turned into yachts, to the lighters that provisioned the ships of Columbus, to the Saxon galleys that brought new settlers to England, to the boat Christ's apostles used to fish the Sea of Galilee, to Charon the ferryman.

SPEEDBOATS

Variously called runabouts, motorboats, sport boats, and ski boats, fast little vessels that exist chiefly for the joy of the ride have been around since the turn of the century. Like sports cars and motorcycles, speedboats are definitely rakish.

On the previous page a fleet of glistening Chris-Craft speedboats from the 1930s and 1940s lines up to be admired and judged for excellence and authenticity at an antique-boat show. Opposite is a two-cockpit Gar Wood runabout from 1937. Boats like these were developed in the Roaring Twenties, built by the tens of thousands, and sold all over the world.

VARIOUSLY CALLED RUNABOUTS, MOTORBOATS, SPORT BOATS, AND SKI BOATS, fast little vessels that exist chiefly for the joy of the ride have been around since the turn of the century. We'll call them speedboats to distinguish them from slower types of motorboats, generally called launches in the United States and Canada, which tend to be more utilitarian. Like sports cars and motorcycles, speedboats are definitely rakish, and their practical uses are for the most part limited to pulling water skiers and winning races. In recent decades, as the antique- and classic-boat movement has flourished with clubs, boat shows, and even a *concours d'elegance* or two in imitation of the classic-automobile hobby, their practical uses have begun to include winning prizes for perfection and authenticity. But speedboats are mostly for fun—for speed!

Speed here means everything from the graceful pace of a mahogany launch with wicker chairs—as much as 25 miles (40 kilometers) per hour and hot stuff for a family boat in 1920—to the 180 miles (288 kilometers) per hour that one of speedboat racing's 1990s Grand-Prix-class boats will achieve over a measured mile. Most of these boats are truly fast—30 to 50 miles (48 to 80 kilometers) per hour—and some of them are classics of their type—old boats that established standards of élan and performance seventy years ago that are still admired in the nineties. The 1916 HackerCraft is arguably the grandmother of all the mahogany speedboats that came along in the twenties and thirties. And there are some brand-new speedboats, modern interpretations

of Jazz Age classics that you can go right out and buy—some of them at prices better than those of their fiberglass counterparts.

HISTORY

There were fast steam launches available to the likes of the Morgans and Vanderbilts before 1900. One of them, a 50-footer (15 meters) owned by the president of Lord & Taylor, was perhaps the fastest boat in America at nearly 27 miles (43 kilometers) per hour in 1888. But speedboats for everybody did not come along until roughly the turn of the century, and then they appeared suddenly all over the place and were available to everybody from clever working-class people who built their own to middle-class cottagers on lakes and rivers. It was the internal-combustion engine that made this happen, just as it made automobiles happen suddenly and ubiquitously between 1900 and 1920. The two phenomena came along at the same time, a result of the engineering free-for-all that started in 1895, when the German patents on the gasoline engine ran out. An example of what was happening is the meeting of two clever men in a Detroit machine shop in 1897. Both were having engine parts made for their backyard projects, and in the machine shop they talked shop and became friends. One was John Hacker, perhaps the world's greatest designer of speed-boats; the other was Henry Ford.

Today's fiberglass sport boats and bass boats are fast, but they are generally not faster than the best of their ancestors. In 1907, a canoe-form displacement hull in America and a pioneer hydroplane in England did better than 30 miles (48 kilometers) per hour. In 1910, a small French hydroplane and a big British racing boat with 760 horsepower both cracked 40 miles (64 kilometers) per hour.

In 1911, another big British raceboat owned by the same English lord and a small hydroplane

A fleet of antique-boat-show competitors hits the throttles in the aerial photo at left. In the lead, appropriately, is an Unlimited-class raceboat from the 1940s. All but the Unlimited are recreational boats capable of speeds to 40 miles (64 km) per hour. The raceboat is capable of more than 100 miles (160 km) per hour. The bow below is typical of the fine craftsmanship associated with wooden boats.

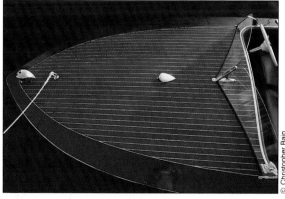

All of the mahogany runabouts of their era— roughly 1920 to 1960—were grand examples of what could be done with varnished wood; but the Greavete Streamliner, shown at right and in detail below, was a tour de force of design and construction. Built from 1936 into the 1950s by Greavette Boats of Gravenhurst, Ontario, Canada, the Streamliner brought 1930s and 1940s industrial-design themes to wooden-boat building.

designed by John Hacker in the United States achieved 50 miles (80 kilometers) per hour. By 1913, updated versions of both British racing boats and John Hacker designs were touching 60 miles (96 kilometers) per hour. By 1920, one of Hacker's hydroplanes was said to be capable of racing-lap speeds better than 65 miles (104 kilometers) per hour, which means it could probably have done 70 miles per hour (112 kilometers) in a straight line on smooth water.

Before 1920, speedboats were specialized items designed and built by hobbyists, motorheads, and local boat shops in places like Wayzata, Minnesota, Alexandria Bay, New York, and Atlantic City, New Jersey. But twenty years after the availability of good little gas engines made speedboats possible in the first place, a huge and cheap supply of good little gas engines made it possible for them to be mass-produced and sold at attractive prices to the general public. The engines were the then-sophisticated aircraft powerplants that had been quickly developed and mass-produced for World War I. After that war, tens of thousands of engines—slathered in Cosmoline,™ more advanced and reliable than the best engines of a decade before, and nicely crated—went on sale at surplus prices.

In the twenties, Horace Dodge bought Curtiss engines for his Dodge line of boats; Gar Wood acquired Liberty engines in whole and in part for his racing machines and for the largest of his stock speedboats; other racing builders bought 200-horsepower Hispano-Suizas; and a family named Smith in Algonac, Michigan, began building boats designed around the war-surplus Curtiss OX-5 engine, rated for 90 horsepower and reported to have cost Chris Smith and his sons only fifty dollars each by the carload.

The Smiths called their boats Chris-Crafts, honoring the old man, and they both defined the type and dominated the powerboat market for decades. As a type, the speedboat is different from every other variety of boat in this book. Sailboats, rowing boats, workboats and even luxury wooden yachts have ancient antecedents and traditions of use. But speedboats are something new. Their parallel history with the automobile has given them something of the aspect of sport automobiles from the antique and classic era—in fact, some of the earliest speedboats were called "autoboats," and the Hacker-designed Belle Isle Bearcats of 1919 were named for the Stutz Bearcat automobile. A boat such as Bill Morgan's replica HackerCraft (or the original of 1929) is like a Packard, Pierce-Arrow, or Cadillac touring car, with pleated leather seats, chrome-plated windshield and trim hardware, and cockpit space for a crowd of passengers enjoying sunlight, scenery, and wind rushing by at 40 miles (64 kilometers) per hour. A boat like the 1929 Nichols launch (a throwback

A classic Gar Wood runabout, Zipalong, above, is more than a showpiece. She spends her summers on the St. Lawrence as an all-purpose vehicle for a vacation home on one of the Thousand Islands, a duty she performs nicely at speeds up to 38 mph.

105

Near the end of the mahogany-runabout era in the United States, in the mid-1950s, Chris-Craft introduced its sleek, finned Cobra model, all varnished wood except for the sculptured rear deck made of something new—fiberglass. Like some of the finned and chrome-trimmed automobiles of the fifties, the Chris-Craft Cobra's aesthetic has held up very well.

© Norman Wangard

© Norman Wangard

to the prewar years) or the 1926 Fay & Bowen with its big cockpit and wicker chairs is like a Model T station wagon—commodious transportation to and from a summer place. The Greavette Streamliner—a rounded sculpture in wood—is like a 1951 Mercury convertible, a flashy ride to have then and now. A Chris-Craft Cobra is almost exactly like a Corvette Stingray in styling and in tooling-around possibilities.

But these are boats, and they are made of wood—and *what* wood! Most of the speedboats shown here are finished bright all over except for bottom paint and a contrasting waterline stripe, and those with painted topsides have lavish expanses of wood on deck and in furnishings and trim. Several varieties of mahogany have always been the wood of choice for these boats, often stained in rich shades of red. *Tartar*, a utilitarian boat for Chesapeake Bay, has only a bit of bright-finished trim; but *Ravelston* is nearly all varnished wood, fitted elegantly in patterns of grain and diagonal joints. It looks like the world's fastest piano.

These are unique vehicles—among the most beautiful boats in the world, indeed among the most exciting boats in the world. Like the Stutz Bearcat and the Corvette Stingray, they are vehicles designed for the joy of the ride and little else. But that's enough on a bright day on a big lake, the engine growling and sending a slight vibration through the wood, the spray flying as the boat chatters through small waves, the wake sweeping astern like the tail of a comet and the wind sweeping over the windshield at 40 miles (64 kilometers) per hour. A fast fiberglass boat can give you a ride like this, but cruising in a wooden speedboat is altogether more satisfying.

LUXURY YACHTS

Of all types of pleasure vessels, luxury yachts in wood come closest to having the atmosphere of a perfectly contrived and specialized little house. A luxurious little house in some ways, a cozy little house in all ways, and a vehicle for escape into another world.

Two of the great luxury yachts of the 1930s are shown on the previous page and opposite. Thunderbird, the amazing creation in the photo on pages 108-109 was designed by John Hacker in 1939 for a wealthy man on Lake Tahoe. Technically a commuter—a luxury cruiser for day trips—she represents Hacker's artistry in bringing 1930s design themes and untraditional materials to boatbuilding. Her gleaming deckhouse is stainless steel. She also represents speed. Her Allison aircraft engines can push her to 70 miles (112 km) per hour.

Shamrock V, opposite, was brought to the United States in 1930 to win the America's Cup. She didn't win, but this first of the 1930s J Boats has been a survivor. Today she sails out of the Museum of Yachting in Newport, Rhode Island.

LUXURY YACHTS MADE OF WOOD ARE NOT USUALLY AS LARGE AND GRAND AS THEIR NONWOOD relatives. Not that the boats in this chapter cannot be defined as luxurious—they are certainly at the more comfortable-and-fancier-than-they-have-to-be end of the spectrum. But most luxury yachts, today and yesterday, have been made of metal and have been more luxurious than any other vehicles in the world. At their smaller scale they traditionally have been at least as luxurious as the castles, mansions and chateaus of the men and women who have been fortunate enough to own them. In fact, they have been nothing less than private cruise ships for an owner and a party of guests accustomed to the atmosphere and services of, say, the Hyde Park Hotel in London. Modern yachting began with the Dutch, who developed fancy versions of their sailing workboats for recreation and for use as floating limousines by officials of their trading companies. The English took up the idea, and by the early 1800s, with the participation of the king, the sport of yachting began to grow in Britain and soon enough on the Continent, in the United States, and nearly everywhere else. Gentlemen took to these boats, that the Dutch called *jachts*, and the English called yachts, for the pleasure and prestige they offered, and the yacht as a type began to evolve.

HISTORY

The great steel and iron steam yachts of Britain and America of a hundred years ago, and diesel yachts of the 1920s that ranged from 100 feet (30 meters) long to ship-size vessels of 400 feet

(121 meters), were incredibly luxurious, but the megayachts launched in the 1980s and 1990s have taken luxury to its limits with restaurant-size kitchens, book-lined libraries, saloons with marble fireplaces, wine cellars, spas with exercise machines and Jacuzzis, and almost anything else you might name or want. Floating palaces like these have never been made of wood.

That's because wood yachts have their limits, and some of these limits defy the addition of certain luxuries. Marble floors, food and beverage service for parties of a hundred, crews of as many as twenty, a dozen staterooms equipped with stereo and video systems—these are really too much luxury for a wooden yacht. If a yacht is to be an escape from Wall Street and Main Street and the Paris Bourse it wants to have the atmosphere of a well-lived-in summer cottage—a comfortable, uncomplicated luxury. The wooden luxury yachts in these pages have that—and it is appropriate. So let us limit our notion of luxury in these pages to what we find here. Is it luxurious? Yes, it is. Is it yachting? Yes, again, in the sense that yachting is an outdoor sport, a change of scene, a situation such as hiking or gardening that puts us in touch with the real world outside our houses and offices.

The luxury yachts in these pages are *a* luxury rather than *the* luxury. It was certainly a luxury in the fifties for my wife's uncle to take his 40-foot (12-meter) mahogany cruiser from upstate New York to Florida and back as an escape from his restaurant business. It was a luxury for John and Marge Pannell to restore John Hay Whitney's great *Aphrodite*, move aboard year-round with their children, and use the boat for cruising and hospitality from Canada to Florida in the eighties. It was a luxury for the Albritton family to acquire *Mykonos*, one of the great Rybovich sportfishing boats, restore it on their own, and enjoy the angling possibilities of South Florida in a boat perfect for the purpose. *Shamrock V* was built as a racing yacht, and Sir Thomas Lipton, an unpreten-

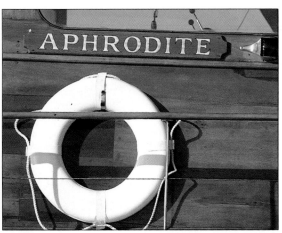

Perhaps the greatest of all the commuters, Aphrodite—*shown in detail above and at full length on the next page—was built in 1937 for John Hay Whitney, who used her to travel from his Long Island estate to Manhattan and for weekend trips to Fisher's Island— luxury transportation, indeed.*

Aphrodite *is a survivor. Discovered rotting away in a boatyard on eastern Long Island in 1983, and restored by John Pannell in his boatyard in Port Washington, Long Island, she looks to be in just-launched condition.* Aphrodite *has been the star of most of the antique-boat shows in the eastern United States during recent summers, and for most of the years since her restoration she has been a floating home for John and Marge Pannell and their children.*

tious man whose tastes ran to comfort more than luxury, kept a ship-sized metal steam yacht called *Erin* for entertaining his guests and for living aboard while his *Shamrocks* were racing. But the last of the *Shamrocks*, a wooden boat, has a certain luxuriousness, from the bird's-eye maple paneling in its saloon to a cozy deckhouse where Sir Thomas and his afterguard could get out of the weather.

One of the things that puts a luxury touch on these yachts is their lavish use of varnished wood. And even when bulkheads and overheads have been painted they have interesting configurations and a flawless finish. The bigger yachts in steel or aluminum always have a lot of wood below decks, and often in structures at deck level, such as pilothouses, benches and settees, varnished

113

A restoration success, Mykonos *was brought back to virtually new condition by the Albritton family of Palm Beach, Florida. A classic and very elite sportfishing boat built by the Rybovich yard in West Palm Beach in 1956, she keeps an active schedule of angling in the Gulf Stream, and she turns heads wherever she goes.*

rails, and spars for flying flags. This lavish use of mahogany and teak, oak, and butternut has "yacht" written all over it, but these big metal boats are just pretending. True wooden yachts have this classic luxury in abundance. They are more yachtlike than the half-size cruise ships made of metal, and their style is appealing to landlubbers and old salts alike, a style that is different from—and arguably better than—that of a house.

Of all types of pleasure vessels, luxury yachts in wood come closest to having the atmosphere of a perfectly contrived and specialized little house. A luxurious little house in some ways, a cozy little house in all ways, and a vehicle for escape into another world. You can move a house like this around, so that tomorrow morning you're standing outside in the sunshine, sipping a second cup of coffee and watching fish swirl the surface of the water under the gaze of pelicans perched in mangroves. Yesterday you were in Miami; this morning you're anchored in Florida Bay and there is not another boat or person in sight. And you got there in your own little house with a pointy end. Down below is a cozy berth, a main cabin with books and musical tapes, a galley stocked with two weeks' worth of food and wine. The world is your oyster. In fact, there are a dozen oysters in the fridge, and in a half an hour or so, if you feel up to it, you may wake your wife with an oyster omelette and some hot croissants for breakfast.

When you look at the photos of the cruising yachts in these pages, you can conjure up such thoughts. Having guests aboard for a cocktail party while tied up in a marina is alright, but these boats are at their best on a cruise—a trip into the wilderness, or what's left of it, with all the comforts of home. So we imagine *Mykonos* on the edge of the Gulf Stream after a three-hour run from Palm Beach and too many cups of coffee adding to the excitement of being out here on an oily swell that gently rocks the boat under whipped-cream clouds. It's a little after ten, the diesels have been

A new classic, Kaiulani was built in 1983 in San Diego to take her adventurous owner on diving expeditions to reefs far into the Pacific. She's a very luxurious world unto herself, a husky schooner yacht with modern machinery and sail-handling gear, and with more than the comforts of home.

shut down, and a dorado has been hooked and lost. There will be more of them. We're out here after sailfish; but dorado are delicious (nobody wants to eat sailfish), and on such a morning it doesn't really matter how well the fishing turns out.

We imagine *Altair* under full sail with a twenty-knot breeze on the beam, heeled over at an angle and with an occasional rogue swell under the bow causing the rigging to clack and shudder and a mist of spray to fly up under the bowsprit. In the late-afternoon sun, the varnish gleams and the wake flashes away from the stern. We are two hours from an anchorage in Ibiza, and who cares if we ever get there?

We imagine *Mer-Na* cruising north from Seattle in the lee of Vancouver Island, all pine forest and

An especially luxurious stock cruiser, Mer-Na
was built by Seattle's Blanchard Boat Company
in 1930. She's a grand example of 1920s and
1930s yacht style, with expanses of varnished
wood and subtle touches of wood trim set off by
white paintwork. She's also a comfortable
floating vacation home for marine
photographer Marty Loken and his family.

© Marty Loken/Allstock

© Marty Loken/Allstock

rocks ashore, a gray, humid day with a promise of fog for tomorrow. A whale breaches far off to starboard, and the skipper has to decide whether to make a side trip to close slowly with what will probably be many whales or to plug along to make port as planned before the long evening of the northern summer ends. A look at the chart and a quick calculation causes him to keep his course. It's satisfying enough to be right here. The old Chrysler Royal is humming along; dinner in a restaurant has been promised to the crew. It is part of the pleasure of cruising to make these decisions about where to go and how to get there.

We imagine *Desperate Lark* at anchor on a late-spring morning, dry and with not much breeze after two days of big blue skies. Time to sand and revarnish the bowsprit and sampson post, which were banged up a little in last season's anchor handling. The owner, sitting on deck sorting out the sandpaper, could have had the boatyard take care of this. But he enjoys doing it himself, anticipating the new China-bristle brush laying down a flawless skin of varnish on the sanded oak.

Wooden boats are an invitation to go cruising—that incalculable pleasure—and they are a responsibility in maintenance, in handling, in cruise planning, and in worrying about how the boat is doing on its mooring an hour's drive from the house the owner occupies reluctantly when life keeps him from his boat. That—as Jon Wilson would say—is a relationship. It is a relationship we do not tend to have with our houses, our automobiles, our golf clubs. It is a relationship that requires more of us than just owning something or doing something. There is something essential about owning a wooden boat, and we can sense it in looking at the photographs in these pages. Maybe it's beauty and truth.

The appropriately named Ragtime *is one of the long, slim, and luxurious commuter yachts built in the 1920s by Consolidated Shipbuilding of New York City to deliver Wall Street millionaires to and from their waterfront estates and their Manhattan offices. This 64-foot (19-m) day boat, built in 1928, is used as a cruising yacht these days, and is one of the few surviving Consolidated Speedway commuters.*

SOURCES

Boat-Building Schools

The Apprenticeshop
Maine Maritime Museum
963 Washington Street
Bath, ME 04530

Bates Vocational and Technical Institute
of Tacoma
Boatbuilding Program
1101 South Yakima
Tacoma, WA 98405

Brookfield Craft Center
PO Box 122
Brookfield, CT 06804

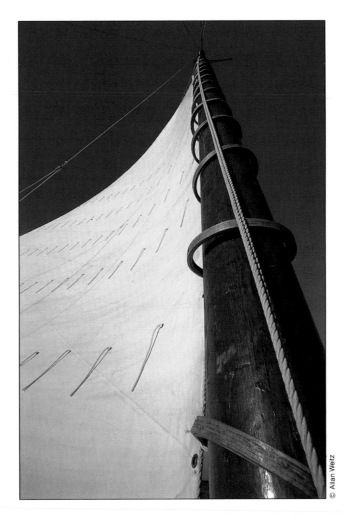

© Allan Weitz

Buffalo State College
Bill Bartoo
Design Dept.
1300 Elmwood Avenue
Buffalo, NY 14222

Cape Fear Community College
David Flagler
411 No. Front Street
Wilmington, NC 28401

The Center for Wooden Boats
1010 Valley Street
Seattle, WA 98109

Chesapeake Bay Maritime Museum

Boatbuilding Courses

PO Box 636

St. Michaels, MD 21663

Cowichan Bay Boatschool

c/o Cowichan Wooden Boat Society

Box 787

Duncan, BC V9L 3Y1

Canada

Duck Flat Wooden Boats

Robert Ayliffe

27 Hack Street

Mount Barker, S.A. 5251

Australia

© Allan Weitz

Falmouth Technical College

Department of Technology

Falmouth, Cornwall, TR11 309

England

Great Lakes Wooden Boat School

Mike Kiefer

227 Prospect

South Haven, MI 49090

International Boatbuilding

Training Centre

Harbour Road, Oulton Broad

Lowestoft, Suffolk, NR323L2

England

SOURCES

James Watt College

William Smith

Finnart Street

Greenock, Scotland

Kingston College of Further Education

Kingston Hall Road

Kingston on Thames

Surrey, England

The Lake Champlain

Maritime Museum

Boatbuilding Courses

Basin Harbor, VT 05491

© Allan Weitz

The Landing School of Boatbuilding

Box 1490

Kennebunkport, ME 04046

Les Ateliers de l'Enfer

Place de l'Enfer

Jean-Jouis Dauga

29 100 Douarnenez,

France

Lowestoft College of Further Education

Department of Construction

& Shipbuilding

St. Peters Street

Lowestoft, Suffolk, NR32 2NB

England

Maine Marine Trades Center

Washington County Technical College

Deep Cove Road

Eastport, ME 04641

Marine Builders' Training School

Hazel Road

Woolston

Southampton S02 7GB,

England

The Marine Museum Boatshop

East Hampton Historical Society

42 Gann Road

E. Hampton, NY 11937

© Allan Weitz

Miami Dade Community College

The Boating Center/South Campus

11011 S.W. 104 Street

Miami, FL 33176

Mystic Seaport Museum

Boatbuilding Courses

Helen Packer, Ships Plans

Mystic, CT 06355

The National Maritime Museum

at San Francisco

Boatbuilding Courses

Foot of Polk Street

San Francisco, CA 94109

S O U R C E S

New Brunswick Community College

Gerald Ingersoll

Boatbuilding Program

PO Box 427

St. Andrews, NB E0G 2X0

Canada

Norfolk School of Boatbuilding

Pier B, Brooks Avenue

PO Box 371

Norfolk, VA 23510

Northwest School of

Wooden Boatbuilding

Glen Cove Industrial Park

251 Otto Street

Port Townsend, WA 98368

The Rockport Apprenticeshop

P.O. Box 539D, Sea Street

Rockport, ME 04856

School For Yacht Restoration

The Museum of Yachting

P.O. Box 129

Newport, RI 02840

Seattle Central Community College

Trade & Ind. Div./Marine Carpentry

23rd Avenue and South Lane

Seattle, WA 98144

South Street Seaport Museum

Boatbuilding Programs

207 Front Street

New York, NY 10038

Southampton College of

Higher Education

Yacht Design/Boatyard Management

East Park Terrace

Southampton, Hampshire,

England

The Sydney Wooden Boat School

River Quays

140 Tennyson Road

Mortlake, N.S.W. 2137,

Australia

© Christopher Bain

The Thousand Islands

Shipyard Museum

Boatbuilding Courses

Bill Smithers

750 Mary Street

Clayton, N Y 13624

University of Alaska at Juneau

Boatbuilding Program

11120 Glacier Highway

Juneau, AK 99801

WoodenBoat School

WoodenBoat Magazine

Rich Hilsinger

PO Box 78

Brooklin, ME 04616